The Designer Life

Distinctions
for Living Life
by Design and
Not by Default

KEVIN KITRELL ROSS
As Seen on the Oprah Winfrey Show

Published in the United States by: Kevin Kitrell Ross

Printed in the United States of America

**For information about special discounts on bulk purchases,
please send inquiries to: designerlife7@gmail.com**

Designed by: Juan Millan of Creave, Inc.
Cover Photo by: Tammy K Photography
Edited by: Seymour Joseph

Library of Congress Control Number: 2012941724

ISBN: 978-0-615-65582-6

2nd Edition, April 2012

*It is Kevin Ross' mission to inspire and empower everyday people to live extraordinary
dreams. To find out more about booking Kevin for speaking engagements or workshops, please visit us at: **www.kevinrossspeaks.com***

To Anita, Angelina, Kameela, and Khaiden,
the great loves of my life. Every day
you show me that the Designer Life
is real and worth sharing with the world.
I love you all!

What people are saying about Kevin Ross...

"On behalf of our fellow Americans, thank you for serving your country. Your commitment as an Americorps volunteer has made America a better place."

– William Jefferson Clinton, Former President of the United States

"Kevin, the energy, passion, and depth that rings through your message are a true reflection of your character. I am reassured that brighter days are ahead because of people like you. Continue to be a powerful voice of compassion, commitment, and truth."

– Father George Clements, Founder & President,
One Church, One Addict, Washington, DC

"Kevin, I am listening to your talk again... Way to go! I love your enthusiasm and how you involve your audience. You are really good... and on your way to becoming one of the great ones!"

– Terry McBride, McBride Enterprises, Mesa, Arizona

"Thank you for the passionate message you shared at the Annual Dr. Martin Luther King, Jr., Summit. You undoubtedly helped in making the tribute an honor to both Dr. King's memory and legacy."

– Cirilio McSween, McDonald's Operators Association, Chicago, Illinois

"Every once in a while, a young woman or a young man comes along that has the spirit of God written all over him or her... and their voice shakes with a passion for Christ. Every once in a while, we who live our lives in service to the poor, to the hungry, to those who are in need, are given a breath of fresh air. I call it a spring moment; a moment of realization that a young man is climbing up the tree of life with the joy of Christ within his very heart. This young man, that I have found to be a part of me, a part of our life, is Kevin. This young man has Christ so large, so profound that his Jesus stands with out-stretched arms embracing all paths and all ways. Truly, Kevin Ross is the 'interfaith child of the 21 st Century'. As I have watched him work, I saw his eyes show the smile that touched his lips. He has taken children from the streets that know no other path other than pain, and brought them to the spirit of God. Any God everywhere, every God anywhere. I salute you, my son, you have brought so many young hopefuls to the spirit of holiness, to the divinity of truth. I cannot wait to hear you preaching to the thousands, to the millions, to bring joy when earth is filled with turmoil, to bring love where hate and bigotry have succeeded in turning youth against youth, man against man, woman against woman. ... I am so proud of the way you embrace all paths... and all ways to your heart. You have made your Christ gigantic in the mind of the young, un-afraid to bring to one's religion. You have given your Christ a form in a child's mind and a space in youth's heart. My God, you are a preacher's preacher. Teach the young how to be young and teach the old to never look back. Live in the mo-ment, my son, your moment filled with Jesus, and teach others how to live in the moment of their own God and their own spirituality. We all will be watching in awe and thankfulness. We all will watch you serve. I love you, Kevin. I have loved you from the day I met you. So you go on and preach God's words and you bring that God to every young person you meet and the world will be great and safer place because Kevin Ross was ordained today."

– Sri Ma Jaya Sati Bhagavati, Kashi Ashram, Sebastian, FL,
presented by Radhe Chan, student of Ma Jaya Sati Bhagavati,
in the Martin Luther King, Jr. International Chapel at Morehouse
College on the occasion of Kevin Ross's ordination into ministry.
April 21, 2002.

Table of Contents

Acknowledgments

Many people have shared in the success of this work. First, I wish to thank my parents, Michael and Janice Ross, for giving me the royal DNA and the unconditional love and support in all my endeavors. They have been right there watching and coaching. Mom, Dad, know that I honor you for giving me permission at a very early age to design my life to be as amazing as I could imagine. Your love, encouragement, and support is the gift that keeps on giving.

Secondly, I wish to honor and thank my grandparents, John and Joyce Tayborn. They are the patriarch and matriarch of our family and so much of my inspiration is drawn from the strength that they have given to their own ten children, forty-plus grandchildren, and eleven great-grandchildren. I take them with me everywhere I go. I promise that no matter where I go I will always know where home is. Also, to my Northside paternal grandmother, Ms. Jimmye Hazel Ross, for always encouraging me to enjoy my life.

No one has had a more profound influence upon my spiritual development than The Reverend Dr. Johnnie Colemon of Chicago's Christ Universal Temple. Without question, she has made such an indelible mark on me that I will never be the same. Having her as my Spiritual Mother, mentor, teacher, friend, counselor and confidante, has helped to open me to my true gifts and has compelled me to step out and let them shine.

My teachers from George M. Pullman Elementary School, and Neal F. Simeon Career Academy, are my true heroes and heroines. I wish to especially acknowledge Mrs. Barbara Powell and Mrs. Margo Baines. From high school, I'd like to thank Mrs. Anna Winters, Ms. Patricia O'leck, Ms. Maxine Soshnik, Ms. Margaret James, Mr. Joel Chaslovsky, and the late Ms. Eleanor Williams, who wrote my letter of recommendation to Morehouse College, and who encouraged me to complete my education.

I am grateful for my journey at Morehouse College, and for all of the professors, counselors and administrators who worked diligently to ensure that we Morehouse men had that something "extra" that the world needs. I am especially grateful to my chief mentor and friend, The Reverend Dean Lawrence Edward Carter, Sr., Dean of Martin Luther King, Jr., International Chapel, who taught me to be ecumenical and to hold my views with tentative confidence.

A special thanks to The Reverend Dr. Joseph Edward Hill, of Chicago's Power Circle Congregation, for seeing the promise in me and having the courage and compassion to officiate at my ordination ceremony. You have always been a pillar of strength and a hidden hand guiding me to become a leader that people can respect and be proud to claim as their own.

To the powerful team that has served alongside me in my many endeavors, from "Kevin Ross Speaks," "Kevin Kitrell

Ross Ministries," "Designer Life Institute," and "Teen Dream Camp," I would like to thank Olivia Benson, Lisa Bromfield, Vern Cameron, Rocio Davis, Kandee G, Crystal Garcia, Gregory Gibbs, David Huerta, Dashanaba King, Aubyn and Sandy Jones, Natalie Knight, Temple McGee, Kathia Ogando, Monikah J. Ogando, Oceana Raye Roman, Brooke and Bob Peterson, David Spearman, Angelique Terrelonge, Yogi Ward and The Reverend Veda Wongchuck.

To The Reverend Dr. Barbara King of Atlanta's Hillsdale International Truth Center, who saw this day coming before anyone else. Thank you for your predicting that this day would come. It inspired me to make it happen.

To Mr. Johnny Regan of "Vision Miami" for giving the "creative class" a place in Miami to share our visions.

To my mentors: The Reverend Dr. Michael Bernard Beckwith, Mr. Les Brown, Dr. Johnetta B. Cole, The Reverend Dr. Frederick J. Eikerenkoetter II, The Reverend Dr. Joseph E. Hill, Mr. Chuck Rankin, the late Sheik Dawud Salahuddin, Mr. Tony Shaw, Mrs. Iyanla Vanzant, and The late Reverend Joanne Wilson.

A special thank you to my friends: Rabbi Shmuley Boteach, Mr. Jack Canfield, Father George Clements, Mr. Randy Gage, Dr. Sorah Dubitsky, Dr. Paul Laughlin, and Mr. Willey Jolley. Each of you has touched a spark within me that inspires me to reach for the stars.

To my closest brother-friends: James Trapp, LeGrande Green, The Reverend Dr. Chris Michaels, David Cook, Leo Alcala,

Jonty Braun, Ralph Campbell, The Reverend Eric Ovid Donaldson, Dr. David E. Montgomery, Dr. David Francis Oliver, Steve Pelmore, Attorney Berve Power, Robert Spicer, and to my baby brothers Michael and Timothy. Every brother needs his "boys." You have been there when I needed you most and I thank you.

To my closest sister-friends: Anna Purna Astley, Radhe Chan, Sita Akaska Griffith, Jo Lena Johnson, Stephanie Jordan Neither, Marshay Artrell Mitchell, Shantilata Stone, Brenda Terry, Deborah Ugarte, and especially my buddy and 3 a.m. friend, Angelique Terrelonge. You are my heroines and my inspiration.

To those who have allowed me to serve them through mentoring: Michelle Delamor, Marlon Barrett, Andres Cortes, Montez Cobb, Kendra Pitman, Alexandria Hernandez, Cheryl Vivieros, and to my students at The Devereaux Center, INROADS, The National Student Leadership Conference and others who have said I touched their lives in some way. This book is for you. Keep letting your lights shine.

To the spiritual community at Christ Unity of Sacramento, thank you so much for welcoming me, my ministry and my family into your hearts and lives. Let these words inspire you to dream and achieve your boldest dreams!

To Seymour Joseph, thank you for taking the time to help edit this work and for your insightful guidance and helpful feedback.

To Juan Millan of Creave and Leo Alcala, thank you for toiling through these pages to lay out this book and to present it in some cohesive form. Thanks for being there to the very end.

To my beloved wife Anita, no one has contributed more than you to seeing to it that this work would be revised and and made available again nine years after its original printing. Thank you for reminding me of the worth of these words and for putting heart, mind, and soul into this project and everything you do!

While it is simply impossible to provide an exhaustive list of everyone who has in some way contributed to my life and this work, know that I am grateful for your love and understanding.

Introduction

"Life is a school, As long as you breathe, you're enrolled."
– Eric Ovid Donaldson

Admit it. You picked up this book, purchased it and have taken it with you because you are ready to make a change. You are ready to upgrade your life and take it to the next level. You are ready to truly anchor your purpose on earth in a way that leaves your indelible signature. You know that you have the goods, because you have tasted those sweet moments when you were in your zone. Yet, there is something addictive about living on purpose all the time, even though it seems like such an effort.

You have been guilty of comparing your life to someone else's and now you have found it is simply a waste of energy because you've discovered that there are no two people alike. This makes you one of a kind! So with this book in your hand, a yearning for more, a self-granted clean slate and the blank canvas of your imagination, we meet.

This intersection in your life is critical. You and I are meeting here to support each other in fulfilling our Divine Assignments. My mission is to inspire and empower everyday people to live extraordinary dreams. And if you're reading this book, you're doing it to receive clarification, guidance, inspiration and motivation to actualize your purpose, and to design a life congruent with your desires. Therefore, our meeting is a perfect match. We will each be in great service to one another.

So this is the part where I break down the title. Here's the title again, *"The Designer Life: Distinctions for Living Life by Design and Not by Default."* In the book *"The Man Who Trapped the Secrets of the Universe,"* Glen Clark quotes the great American achiever Walter Russell, the subject of the book, as having said the following: *"The successful man is one who is considered to have made a success of his life according to modern standards, which include the accumulation of money, properties, and an honorable place in the world for notable achievement and financial worth. In other words, the successful man is generally conceived as being one who accumulates values which can be rated by Bradstreets'. But there is something still greater than all of that, there is the Life Triumphant which transcends all material success. The Life Triumphant is that which places what a man gives to the world in creative expression far ahead of that which he takes from it of the creations of others."*

So, the Designer Life is less about what you can accumulate materially, but more about what you can contribute with your gifts. When you learn to design a life that's congruent with your authentic desires, that's aligned with your purpose and that projects your gifts meaningfully into the world, then you will automatically attract to you a lifestyle where no good thing is left out. Yes, an extraordinary life!

To break you out of living by default — how it's always been, how others predict it to be for you, and society's lowest expectation of you —, I have outlined below the Five Core Designer Life Distinctions. These distinctions are principles that will support you in living the Designer Life. Refer to them often and use them as guidelines to keep you on track for the inevitable fulfillment and success that comes with being a conscious life designer.v

1. The Designer Life is a life of purpose.

While this may seem to be stating the obvious, it is worth mentioning. Walter Russell, in his quote mentioned earlier, referred to what may be paraphrased as empty measures of success. But don't get me wrong. The Architect of the Universe engineered each one of us to prosper. So, as you design your life, you shouldn't ignore material prosperity, such as money and whatever values that enhance your enjoyment of your chosen lifestyle. Actually, it is impossible to do so because the natural result of a life of purpose is prosperity, or growth. Abundance will come your way the moment you have a purpose that focuses primarily on serving the world, not on serving yourself. When you are on purpose, you frequently cross-examine yourself with the question, *"Is this choice I am about to make aligned with my greater purpose for being on the planet?"* This simple question will save you lots of pain and hours wasted on unfulfilling activity. When you are living on purpose, you live your life with an assurance that *"I will be guided in all of my affairs."* In fact, you will learn to move forward with the impulse that your actions will make a difference.

2. The Designer Life is a spiritual life.

To design the life of your dreams, you must first have a dream, or a vision for your life. This requires that you reach beyond mere three-dimensional living, beyond seeing yourself as a mere human being. You are more than human, you are divine. That is, you are one with the Living Intelligence that governs the universe. When you live with this awareness, you harness the creative faculties within you, as well as those creative energies that lie all around you. In so doing, a dynamic interaction ensues. No longer are you bound to limited circumstance, you are empowered to create the conditions that change circumstance into opportunity. You become an alchemist who is not fooled by the illusions of obstacles and stumbling blocks. These are "disturbances in the force," contradictions that need to be weighed and overcome. Properly confronted, these occurrences help to support you with your own evolution. In this way, life is not happening to you, life is happening for you. Thus, when you are living the Designer Life, you do so ever conscious of your connection to Spirit. You recognize that your life is a constant relay of information and impulse between you and the Spirit. Every masterpiece of art, for example, is a Divinely Intended, Humanly Permitted collaboration.

The more confidence you have in the invisible and intangible, the more mastery you will have over the tangible and visible dimensions of life.

3. The Designer Life is a no-excuse life.

To offer excuses is to disarm yourself of your creativity, imagination, will, power, responsibility and your Divine connection. This is tough because, as the Designer, everything showing up in your life is by your own design. It's tough because some things that show up in our lives we would never arrange for consciously. We are more than the bodies we inhabit and are connected to the whole of life. Consciously or not, we play our role in all of life's amazing events. Some of them appear to be positive, some negative. Those that appear negative, however, may not be negative after all. I have had the privilege of observing artists paint. From time to time they create something they consider less than satisfactory. Yet they never blame someone or something for the result; they simply set up a new canvas. The designer should never be limited to this or that design. If what you have designed is not the masterpiece you were hoping for, go back to the drawing board. You always have the option to start anew. To live the Designer Life means you are willing to take 100% responsibility 100% of the time for the life you're leading. It is this self-awareness that empowers you to design and redesign your life. Excuses are the coward's way of sidestepping responsibility.

4. The Designer Life is a life of enjoyment.

If you believe that life is only filled with struggle, pain, disappointment and hardship, you have a choice to make. You can either suspend that belief for now and read on, or you can hold on to your negative feelings about life. If you choose the latter, you may just as well give this book to someone who is ready to start living. Living is not a matter of breathing in and breathing out. A properly designed life is filled with joy, fun, adventure, excitement and bliss. You must find a way to include some play time into your days of work and duty. You must design your life in such a way that memories of days gone by will warm your heart. In your planning, goal-setting — even your dreaming — you should try to visualize yourself smiling, laughing, loving, and being loved. See and feel yourself excited, elated, enthused. See and feel yourself having the time of your life. Learn to ask yourself the question, *"How could I be enjoying this moment even more than I am right now?"* Stay open for the response, then act upon it. Joy is when a person has found his or her *why* for living.

5. The Designer Life is the Life Triumphant.

This is the life where the life designer is victorious over circumstances, a positive transformer of community and a leader in society. It is a life where you win each day because you are living a life built on your values, in conformity with your desires, in service to your purpose, in harmony with your fellowman, and in love with life itself. In fact, the secret behind it all is love! You are most triumphant when you are suspended in a moment where you are living the life you love and loving the life you live. It is in such a life that you welcome living in creative tension; your desire for more is constantly rubbing against the appearance of "not enough". Notice I said it is the *appearance* of "not enough." If you are willing to release your creative impulses, they will dissolve those feelings of "not enough." When you live in response to this impulse and answer the longing of your heart, you are triumphant because you have demonstrated your power to use your life as a solution to the pressing demands of the world.

Now it is time to delve deeper into the revelations waiting for you in the pages of this book. The wisdom gathered and compiled for you is a culmination of a lifetime of study, mentoring, and practice. Some of you will be familiar with some of what you read. In fact, this book is rather "Oprahesque." I am honored to say that I was presented on the Oprah Winfrey Show, as "Oprah's Ultimate Male Viewer", because my life's work aligns with the ideas and ideals Oprah Winfrey represents in her programs. She is indeed living her life's calling, a calling that has made her one of the most successful people in the world.

I am also proud to be given the "Oprah's Ultimate Male Viewer" title because every principle and technique I share in this book are the very ones I employed to become an

Here I am at the Oprah Winfrey Studio show studio after achieving one of my life-long dreams of being an invited guest on the Oprah Winfrey Show.

invited guest to pay tribute to Oprah on the historic farewell episode taped at the United Center in Chicago before 13,000 fans and aired before millions around the world. I want you to be intrigued enough, inspired enough, and curious enough to say to yourself, *"If Kevin Kitrell Ross can do it, so can I!"*

My desire is that you put this book to the test. Write in it. Highlight in it. Underline and circle things that stand out for you. Move into it. As an artist's studio is rarely spic and span, so should be your approach to this book. Be messy with it. Ingest each idea, or "mind-seed," you come across. The ideas and tools in this book are practical. I know they work because I have worked them, as have countless others. Now it' s your turn. It's your time to shine. Use this book to put you on the path to living the Designer Life everyday. You deserve it. The world is waiting for you, so get started!

Kevin Kitrell Ross
February 2012
Sacramento, California

Notes:

Notes:

1

Your Designer Genes

―――(")―――

*"Power undirected by high purpose
spells calamity; and high purpose but itself
utterly useless if the power to put it
into effect is lacking."*
– Theodore Roosevelt

*"I may not know what purpose is, but I know
what it is not, and that's keeping busy in the
thick of thin things, consuming valuable space,
air, and time that a more focused person
could be using."*
– Kevin Kitrell Ross

―――(")―――

What on Earth Am I Here To Do?

As a spiritual teacher, coach and radio show host, I find that more often than not the greatest source of frustration that people have comes from feeling that they have no idea why they are on the planet. Most of my hours in coaching and counseling are spent with people unaware that they were born with designer genes. That is, they have within them a perfect pattern or an inner code that will lead them to the manifestation of a life of meaning, contribution, and fulfillment. Without an awareness of this, people spend a great deal of their lives living out everyone else's design but their own.

Many of their personal challenges stem from not living a life which reflects their authentic desires. Consequently, they find themselves meandering through life aimlessly, hoping to hit some target or other, rather than identifying a target and going for it completely. There is a saying, *"If you don't know where you are going any road you take will get you there."* The problem does not lie in not knowing what road to take. The problem lies in not stopping to ask for directions. If this sounds like you, then use this book to direct you to the path of your purpose.

The Answers Are Closer than You Think

Suffering results from idleness and not having a meaningful and fulfilling outlet to direct one's life. Health challenges, depression, insomnia, addiction, poor finances, among other countless problems, are the result of living the life void of purpose. Why? Within the soul of each person is a gift uniquely his or her own. It is in the unwrapping of this gift that life's most essential questions get answered. Unfortunately, too few people recognize that their salvation is found within, not without. Each of us must seek to satisfy that innate craving for meaning. Without any clear direction — like Dorothy in the Wizard of Oz — we search for "home" in a far off place, only to discover that what we had been seeking was with us all along. The key is to start your search by looking within.

Are People Really Clueless?

I think not! Cluelessness suggests that a person hasn't the faintest notion about the direction he or she should take in life. Every person has a clue — and, yes, that includes you. I have found that the most common issue is that many of us live our lives afraid of our potential. Simply put, we are afraid that we *can* actually have it all, even a career that we are passionate about.

Somewhere along the way, we learn that our chosen career holds some intrinsic worth. We become enrolled in the idea that what we do has more value than who we are. To that end, we frequently choose a path that seems to have more societal value than that which brings personal fulfillment. My intention with this section is to prompt you to become extremely honest with yourself and to make it safe for you to accept what rings true for you, as it pertains to the path that you take.

Even if the path you must take is a lonely one, it will be rewarding because it will ultimately lead you to expressing your most
authentic self. It is in doing so, that the doorway to your potential is kicked wide open and the journey of a lifetime will ensue.

From the time a child can talk and begins to form his or her
personality, clues begin to appear. Parents, relatives and loved
ones, after observing the child in action, begin to suggest what
they see as the child's potential. "Look at our little doctor,"
says a proud father. "She's always got something to say, she's
bound to be an attorney," says a mother. Or how about when
you were a child and each day you came home from school
with a new declared career? Do any of these sound familiar:
"Mommy, I want to be a fireman!", "Daddy, I want to be a singer!", "Grandma, I want to be a basketball player!", "Grandpa,
I want to be a teacher!" I know I have encountered this with
many children and even my young daughters have begun their
declarations.

So what happens to us between childhood and adulthood that
makes us lose our sense of the unlimited possibilities for ourselves and go searching for answers in books such as this one?

Our Unconscious Inheritance

Each person is born an heir. You are an heir, whether you are
conscious of it or not. Most of us are not conscious of our heri-
tage and wonder how we got to be the way we are. The family you were born into, the neighborhood you grew up in, the
school you attended, and the people who had early influence

on you, are all part of your unconscious inheritance. The attitudes, values, mindsets and beliefs of our parents are passed down to us.

Far too often, however, we inherit attitudes and behaviors that are detrimental to guiding us in the right direction. This happens so frequently because we live in a world that fosters in us a dependence on the views, ideas, philosophies, trends, and opinions of others. The extent to which we have allowed ourselves to be conditioned to relying on the external views and ideas of others, without contemplating and connecting with what feels highest and best for us on an individual level, we unconsciously participate in the erosion of our own self confidence.

We then waste much of our adult lives trying to "unlearn" this limiting, negative programming. For example, the old saying that children should be seen but not heard is still very much alive in many families. We inherit a false idea of what a child's place should be. We learn that children shouldn't question their parents. Some of us grew up in households where, in a sense, we were our own parents. We lacked guidance, and consequently lost our grip on the true meaning of life.

Our society tells us it's okay not to know your purpose during your early childhood. *"Use the time to just be a child,"* it suggests. Studies show that children are most imaginative in their formative years and are therefore most daring, unafraid, and open to experiencing with their gifts and talents, exploring their potential and discovering their purpose. There is no better time for us to get a sense of our purpose than when we are children, because we are too inexperienced to know about failure. The Master Jesus taught *"Except ye be converted, and become as little children, ye shall not enter into the kingdom of heaven"* (Matthew 18:3, KJV).

Ultimately, I want you to dance with the doubt, the fear and the uncertainty that appears in your life. Rather than avoiding it, facing it will awaken in you the creativity, develop the inner strength, and build the courage it takes to design a life that you will be proud to call your own.

Recapture Your Innocence

There is a well-known story that has been circulated through the internet about a three year old boy who went into a nursery to visit his newborn baby sister. When he was sure no one was listening, he peeked over her crib and said to his sister, *"Please tell me what God looks like, because I am beginning to forget."* There is an untouched place of innocence within each of us that has not been affected by our socialization, is fearless of any challenge, and still remembers what the voice of God sounds like. Returning to this place is the starting point in our journey toward self-discovery. In our later years, the impulse to dream, travels through so much toxic programming that we often have to unlearn our way to success. You must try to recapture that innocence, that spiritually unadulterated place in you that is fully awake and connected to God's original purpose for your life. It's still there. Seek with all of your heart and you will find it.

Know Thyself: Who Am I Really?

"The purpose of life is undoubtedly to know oneself. We cannot do it unless we learn to identify ourselves with all that lives. The sum total of that life is God. The instrument of this knowledge is boundless, selfless service."

– Mohandas K. Gandhi

"Therefore, since we are the offspring of God, we ought not to think that the Divine Nature is like gold or silver or stone, something shaped by art and man's devising."

– Acts 17:29

Let's get down to it. You are eager and you are tired of not knowing your purpose. You've asked everybody there is to ask. You've taken every course there is to take. You've purchased every self-help book and tape series there is to purchase. You've gone to every seminar and you've heard every sermon and you've picked up this book with a powerful resolve to get it or quit it! Ready for the answer? Here it is: Your purpose in life is to express God!

Yes! That's it. Of course there's more to it than that, but not much more. As the ancients have been known to say, self-knowledge is the key to the mystery of mysteries. Knowing who you are is imperative to discovering your purpose. In fact, who you are IS your purpose. We are all here to be ourselves. For a moment, suspend your past programming and what you have been conditioned to believe to be true about yourself. Allow yourself to receive a new thought that just may revolutionize your life. Ask yourself the question, *"Who am I?"* Do it. Do it now! Give yourself a moment to experience what comes to you. Notice the immediate responses that come to mind and the sensations you feel in your body. Now think this: *"I am an idea in the mind of God."* You might also put it this way: *"I am a blueprint in the mind of God."*

Does this come as a surprise to you? Perhaps you may not believe in God. But, supposing that God does exist, wouldn't it be wonderful to know that you are a masterpiece created by the Architect of the Universe? That would be much greater than if you were a painting by Monet, or a play by Shakespeare. Greater, yes, to be a creation of the mind of God! God thought you up! God had something very specific in mind when God was thinking of you. And who can question the height of God's standards?

This leads to the question, "How do I discover what idea I am in the mind of God?" We'll get to that in a minute. First, let's learn a little about the nature of God and our relationship to God. As William Herschel said, *"There can be no self-understanding without God-understanding."*

Here's a viewpoint that may enhance your understanding of God, so that you may accelerate your own self-understanding. Charles Fillmore, co-founder of the Unity School of Practical Christianity, and a writer on the subject of our divine potential, points out in his book, *Dynamics for Living*, *"The starting point in spiritual realization is a right understanding of God. God is the absolute, incomparable All Good, the principle of divine benevolence that permeates the universe. God is Spirit, the Principle of creative life, the moving force in the universe, the omnipotent, omnipresent, essence from which all things proceed. The firstborn of everything in the universe is an idea in Divine Mind. In God Mind an idea is the original, primary, or unlimited thought of Being. Ideas may be combined in a multitude of ways, producing infinite variety of forms."*

By understanding the spiritual, absolute good, unlimited, all-powerful nature of God, we get a glimpse of our origins and our potential. Like you and I, God wishes to fulfill God's self. One of the ways that the Infinite gets to fulfill Itself is by clothing Itself in a multitude of finite forms. Highest of all creation is humanity. In the Bible and other holy texts, humanity is the only one in creation that is made in the image and likeness of God. That is, in creation God has placed Itself in humanity as Its own radiant, magnificent reflection. So, figuratively speaking, God looks into creation for humanity to mirror back unto Itself all of its attributes, characteristics, and powers. Therefore, the seed of potential that is within each one of us is destined Godward. For example, the offspring of a cat is a kitten. The offspring of a dog is a puppy. So what becomes of the offspring of God? Here is what the Psalmist David says of us: *"I have said, Ye are gods; and all of you are children of the most High"* (Psalms 82:6). You may be thinking that that's an Old Testament text, they are not the words of Jesus. But here's what The Master Teacher Jesus said, quoting the ancient Hebrew text, *"Jesus answered them, Is it not written in your law, I said, Ye are gods?"* (John 10:34) So what is the offspring of God? The answer is a god. Yes, you!

Spiritually, our potential is to be like God. We have this capacity, and express it when each of us learns to evolve from what has been involved. That is, we are to express what has been impressed. And impressed in the heart of every person is his or her God potential which originated in the mind of God. Our task is to find it and unleash it.

Some Good News About You as an Idea

The late Ralph Bunch, political scientist and diplomat, had a favorite saying, *"If you want to get across an idea, wrap it up in a person."* Wrapped up in you is an idea that holds the seed to your destiny. This seed holds the key to your Divine Design. Among the definitions of an idea that Webster offers, some stand out: *"A plan of action, an intention, a mental image, a figure."* If an idea is an intention and you are an idea in God's mind, then it follows that you were meant to be! Likewise, the idea that you represent in the mind of God is the plan of action that is your life. This plan is not an architect's blueprint. It is, however, like a scroll, the contents of which are only revealed as it unravels. Your life is a figure of God's imagination, and has the characteristics of that imagination. There are boundless possibilities for your growth without limitation. God knows you and is constantly dreaming up new worlds of possibility for you. As Oprah Winfrey said as she addressed the Morehouse College graduating class of 1999 (my graduating class), *"God can dream a bigger dream for you, so let God dream that big dream through you."*

Ideas are the Total Package

"Every child born into the world is a new thought of God, an ever-fresh and radiant possibility."
– Wiggin

In his book, *"Atom Smashing Power of the Mind,"* Charles Fillmore tell us *"The ideas of Divine Mind are whole and complete in their capacity to unfold perpetually greater and more beautiful forms according to the thinking capacity of man."* This means that each of us arrived on the planet totally equipped with all that we will ever need to fulfill our purpose. We are fully endowed with every attribute necessary to bring forth our purpose and to manifest our greatest potential. So if you think you are missing something, or that you are not enough, it is only because you have been measuring yourself by false standards, and not by your true spiritual nature. When you need encouragement, affirm to yourself, *"I am the perfect expression of the perfect idea. I am the total package!"*

Perhaps it seems like a tall order to be told that your purpose lies as an idea in the mind of God. But this is not as difficult as it may seem. For example, after I completed the process I will outline for you, I discovered that I am the idea in the divine mind of empowerment. When God dreamed me up, God imagined me as being a vehicle through which God empowers people. My purpose, therefore, is to empower people to be victorious over circumstances, to be positive transformers of community and leaders of society. By teaching and modeling the universal spiritual principles for personal empowerment and global transformation, by realizing that I am here as an agent of empowerment and by coupling my skills and gifts with this idea, I live a rewarding and effective life.

Here are some tried and tested ways to zero in on the idea that you are in divine mind:

1. Ask God to tell you

This is the most direct route and you will be amazed how simple yet profound this can be. The Biblical scripture assures us, *"If any of you lack wisdom, let him ask of God, that giveth to all men liberally, and upbraided not; and it shall be given him"* (James 1:5). Begin this exercise by being perfectly still in a quiet place where you can concentrate. Get in a comfortable relaxed position. Take a few deep breaths and imagine yourself entering into the mind of God. Now gently whisper to God your question. You might say, *"Dear God, what is my unique purpose? How do you wish to express your life as me?"* Now sit silently in the mind of God and listen for a response. If you feel such a response, in the spaces below take a moment and write down what you feel God has revealed to you. You may have to try this a second, or even a third time, before you feel a Godly answer to your question.

_____

_____

_____

_____

_____

2. Define your desires

What you desire provides clues into what you are here to express. I am speaking of desire in the original meaning of the word, which comes from the Latin: de, which means "of," and sire, which means "Father." Thus, your true desires are "of" the "Father," or of God. Therefore, whatever it is that you seem to be longing or craving to express, it is simply God wishing to express it through you. What are your desires? What is it that you are hungering for? What do you feel impelled to attain?

Write it down here.

_____

_____

_____

_____

_____

3. Check your equipment

Rupert said, *"A buried talent is never a buried treasure. Talents become treasures only through use."* Your equipment is comprised of your gifts, talents, and skills. In some way or other, your equipment provides clues to your unique purpose. For example, if you purchased an airplane, its aerodynamically engineered body, wings, engines and fuel would give us an idea of the functionality of the vehicle. Given its equipment, its "purpose," as a mode of transportation, is to fly.

You have special gifts, talents and skills that will indicate what your functionality should be. While your equipment may serve as an indicator, it should not become a limitation to what you can achieve. Below are some working definitions you may use to assist you in realizing the subtle distinctions between gifts, talents and skills on the lines below. Yes! I want you to keep writing in this book. Use this book as your tool for personal empowerment and transformation.

Gifts: Those God-given abilities you did not have to work for, in order to gain. For example, I am a gifted speaker. For as long as I can remember, I have been able to speak eloquently.

Talents: Your power of mind or body that gives you the capacity for achievement or suc-   cess. Different from a gift, your talent is that special ability you have that you intend to use to bring you success. For example, a talented singer is intended to use his or her voice to uplift the world and not merely sing in the shower. My mentee Michelle Delamor is a talented vocalist and through the cultivation and development of her tal-

On the set with my mentee, Teen Dream Camp graduate, and American Idol Season 9 finalist Michelle Delamor.

ent, she placed in the top 20 of American Idol, where she touched millions with her voice.

Skills: A craft, trade, job or special aptitude requiring manual dexterity or special training, in which you have competence. For example, typing is not a talent or a gift for me. It is a skill that I acquired as a high school student through study and practice.

As you review the inventory of your equipment, do you notice attributes that point to your functionality? When I do this exercise, I realize that I have a God-given "gift for gab." Being given that gift, I conclude that it must be God's intention for me to use speech as a major part of my life's purpose. I was built for it. What were you built for? The next question I asked myself was, *"What am I to speak about, or for whom shall I speak?"* These questions helped me to dig out my passion. Your passion is a cause or a group that you feel strongly committed to serving, learning from or positively impacting. Likewise, you may feel equally opposed to, want to eradicate, protest against or dismantle a group or cause.

Let's break down the word passion shall we? P-A-S-S-I-O-N. Now I am going to group it differently. PASS-I-ON. Yes, you see it. If I simply added the letter T to this grouping of words, I would have a sentence, "PASS-IT-ON." Your passion is that part of you that is contagious, that cannot be held back. You must share it. You must pass it on. This is something that you are enthused by. Enthusiasm is a Greek compound word that means "en theos" or "in God". Again, like your desire, your passion is God-directed and God-sustained. Laurie Beth Jones, in her outstanding book, *"The Path,"* offers us several causes from which to select to assist us with narrowing down our passion.

4. Pick Your Passion

From the list below, circle three causes that most attract you:

Agriculture	Family Issues	Nutrition
Administration	Fashion	Parks and Recreation
Animal Care	Finance	Performing Arts
Poverty	Animal Conservation	Food
Politics	Animal Rights	Gardening
Art	Government	Printing and Publishing
Biotech	Health Care	Public Safety
Books	Home Health Care	Real Estate
Border Issues	Homeless	Religion
Broadcasting	Human Development	Reproductive Issues
Business	Ill and Disabled	Research
Child Care	Immigration	Roads and Bridges
Child Protection	Infants	Sexuality Issues
Children	Journalism	Space Exploration
Churches	Justice	Spirituality
Civil Rights Issues	Justice System	Sports
Computer Technology	Labor Relations	Substance Abusers
Community Action	Law	Synagogues
Education	Construction	Literacy
Tourism	Design	Management
Travel	Defense	Media
Veterans	Movies	Water
Elderly	Music	Women's Issues
Energy	News	Youth
Environment	Non-profit Agencies	Rights

5. Partner Your Passion with Your Purpose

Rhonda is a gifted artist. She was inspired one day, feeling an urge to paint. She went to the craft store and bought a canvas, paint and paintbrushes. Prior to this she had never painted before. She went home that evening and realized that she left the paintbrushes at the store. All she had was a canvas, some paint, and a plastic paint mixer. But her desire to paint was unstoppable, so she took the plastic paint mixer and went at it. She painted the most beautiful African mask you ever saw. No one would have believed that she did this without a paintbrush. They certainly wouldn't believe that she had never painted before. The story gets better.

Over time, Rhonda accumulated a "private collection" of her paintings. I call it private because she rarely let anyone see it. She kept it to herself. Does this sound like you? Is there a hidden talent that you aren't sharing with the world? After seeing her collection, I encouraged her to host an art show. I promised to assist her with making the arrangements for the event. Initially, she wouldn't hear of it. She told me that I was biased and that other people would not like her paintings as much as I did. Finally, I convinced her that she could do it and that people would like her work. She didn't know what to charge for her art, and she didn't just want to have an art show to sell paintings. She wanted her art show to make a difference. She had a passion for children, so she decided to have a "Silent Art Auction" to benefit a youth organization. The art show and auction was a huge success. And while there's nothing wrong with earning money, using your gifts and talents to benefit those causes dear to you, as well as yourself, is the most gratifying thing imaginable.

That is exactly what my friend did. She partnered her purpose with her passion. Her purpose was to express her artistic gifts through painting. Her passion was to benefit disadvantaged youths. When she connected them, something amazing happened. In her very first auction, entitled, "Undisturbed Harmony," she sold over 80 percent of her collection. No painting sold for under $150.

She donated a portion of the profit to her favorite charity, an organization that flies third and fourth graders from inner city public housing projects to spend a weekend on a college campus to get an early experience of higher education.

Rhonda's passion inspired her to work harder to develop her gift. She became so competent that people were clamoring to purchase her work even paintings that were not for sale.

After fifteen years as a flight attendant, Rhonda unleashed her true passion as an artist and today she enjoys a full-time career as a visual artist and photographer. And she has inspired several others to tap into their unlimited potential, pick up paintbrushes and paint their way to success. This is what happens when you partner your passions with your purpose. You inspire and empower others to do the same. Marianne Williamson's brilliant words in her best-selling book, "*A Return to Love*," summarizes this point precisely:

"Our deepest fear is not that we are inadequate.
Our deepest fear is that we are powerful beyond
measure. It is our light, not our darkness, that
most frightens us. We ask ourselves, 'Who am
I to be brilliant, gorgeous, talented, fabulous?'
Actually, who are you not to be? You are a child
of God. Your playing small doesn't serve you,
shrinking so that other people won't feel insecure
around you. We are all meant to shine, as children
do. We were born to make manifest the glory of
God that is within us. It's not just in some of us;
it's in every one. As we let our light shine, we
unconsciously give other people permission to do
the same. As we're liberated from our own fear,
our presence automatically liberates others."

6. Analyze Your Aptitude

Earlier I defined a skill as being a craft, trade, job, or a special aptitude requiring manual dexterity or special training in which you have competence and experience. As you search to uncover the idea in Divine Mind that you best express, you can gain some insight into this by looking at the skills you have chosen to develop. Those of us who feel that we are not doing what we were meant to do may be doing some semblance of it. Before you count yourself out, take a look at what skills, professional training and experience you have accumulated over the years. There is a reason why you gravitated to a particular area of study and practice.

While some of us may follow a clear outline of training for a specific career, others may have acquired certain skills in an experiential fashion. This is how some people end up becoming a jack-of-all-trades, but master of none. Yet there is hope for you. Having many skills is good because it will give you a wider range to choose the one you wish to master.

For example, my dear friend Eric Donaldson went to college to study business. He later went on to become the marketing director for a major retail chain. Following this, he attained printing and layout experience as a copy technician at Kinko's. Finally, Eric founded his own motivational speaking and training company.

Eric has numerous skills: business, organization, printing, writing, marketing, ministerial, computer, and public speaking. He could have chosen any one of these areas as a career. However, — and here's the key — Eric has pulled from the best of each of these skills to support his passion. Eric went on to become an ordained minister and served as the National

Executive Director of One Church, One Addict. He used his writing skills to develop proposals for grants. He used his copy and layout skills to oversee the production of reports, presentations, brochures and materials. He used his public speaking gifts in his many talks on recovery across the country. He used his ministerial training to aid him as a pastor and spiritual counselor to those in the recovering community.

Today, Eric similarly applies his gifts, talents and skills as the Senior Minister of Unity Christian Church of Memphis and traveling the country with a Healing Workshop that he created. When he began his search for a career, he probably did not expect to be where he is today. Clearly, he did not follow a straight line to discovering his purpose. It was a process. While you may not be able to detect where you are or what your value is, trust the process.

I like to refer to Eric's process as the baseball approach to self-discovery. While a pitcher's main competence is throwing a baseball sixty-feet-six-inches, he has to be somewhat proficient in every aspect of the game. For example, after he releases the ball he automatically becomes a fielder. He also has to know how to cover the bases and catch fly balls in the outfield, just in case he is called upon to play one of those positions. He must know the rules of the game — especially the strike zone. In other words, while he is mainly "at home" on the pitcher's mound, he has to have a comprehensive competence for the entire game of baseball.

I can draw another parallel with the role of Coach. Though a person may have played every position on the team and played them well, coaching may prove to be his best asset. But having that experience playing the game, would make him a much more effective coach.

All this to say that, sooner or later, your skills and experiences will reveal their secrets to you.

7. Be Practical

Save time, needless pain and anxiety, by being realistic with your quest. You may have your heart set on accomplishing one thing, while your skills will enable you to excel in another. For example, while I like mathematics and science, I have a greater attraction to, and mastery of, words and language. Let us keep our lives free of complication by developing ourselves in the areas that we both enjoy and can commit to. Don't "sign up" for something for which you don't possess the competency.

It makes no sense whatsoever to apply for medical school if you know that you don't like studying and have an aversion to seeing and handling body tissue and blood. Why become an accountant when you perform poorly in math? This doesn't mean you shouldn't challenge yourself in an area of weakness. Striving to overcome is the noblest sign of healthy character. But you shouldn't frustrate yourself to the point of despair. I recommend that you move in the direction in which you are best predisposed and allow your gifts, talents and skills to support you in your pursuit. In short, "go for what you know." Life is too short and unpredictable to use your time focusing on the "thick of thin things."

Work to hone your skills to help you move forward in your chosen direction. While you already possess certain skills, those you choose to acquire should be practical. They should be the tools that will bring you the joy that comes with being on purpose.

8. Take a Poll

Someone has aptly said, *"You are not other people's opinion."* Although we all have people in our lives whose opinions we value, it does not mean we are to allow the opinions of others to define who we are or to determine the choices we make. It does, however, mean that we are open-minded enough to survey a range of viewpoints to inform our choices.

Who should these people be and what questions should we ask? A person's chief advisors do not necessarily have to be friends or family. Far more important are relationships based on a shared vision. In surrounding ourselves with those who will share our vision, it is important that we don't merely select based upon shared DNA or a length of time that we have known an individual. It is important that we also have a shared vision. A vision is an image of a preferable future. There is power in aligning yourself with someone who shares your vision. They are more likely to encourage you, energize you, champion you, and celebrate with you. Another secret of having a shared vision is that doing so is synergistic and as such amplifies, accelerates and magnetizes your dream for exponential success! These relationships are indispensable. You may foster such relationships with colleagues and professors from academic institutions, fraternity or sorority friends, co-workers, people from your church or your chosen spiritual tradition. Nevertheless, the people whose advice you seek should always have your best interests at heart.

Here I am with my spiritual partner, Best Selling Author, Gary Zukav.

Half of winning in life is asking the right people the right questions. Here are some questions to ask your closest advisors, as you seek to gain clarity on your purpose:

1. Given what you know about me, what do you see are my strengths and weaknesses?

2. Of my talents, are there some that stand out more than others?

3. What do you think would be the best use of my skills?

4. What cause do I strike you as being most passionate about?

5. When you think of me, is there anything you feel I am not cut out for?

6. When do you think I shine the most?

7. When have you noticed me shining the least?

8. What would you say is my calling or unique purpose in life?

9. What would you suggest I do to move in the direction of my purpose?

10. Can I count on you to support me with your unconditional love and constructive feedback as I design a life worth having?

Loyal friends will take the time to listen and give you sincere feedback on these questions. Make it worth their while. Consider treating the person to lunch and having this discussion. You may also opt to meet in a public library or in a classroom, somewhere the two of you can have uninterrupted focus and concentration. Show the person that you really value his or her responses by taking notes. People are more eager to share their thoughts when they feel they have a receptive audience.

Later, when you have the time, consider their responses. Weigh their comments and suggestions against what you feel to be true about yourself. Look for points of agreement, as well as points of difference. You may find a hidden nugget of truth in one of those differences. You may have a blind spot in self-estimation which your friend has hit upon. Such confidences and observations deserve careful consideration. Remember, what you are seeking is seeking you!

9. Fail at trying something

Are you shocked at this suggestion? This does not sound like the advice you would expect to get from a self-help book. But if the truth be told, most successes are built on failures. We can all relate to watching a baby take those awkward first steps. We watch the first attempt and then the fall and then the second attempt and then the fall. The lesson in this is that it doesn't matter how many times the baby falls; the true measure of success is how many times the baby gets back up.

If you're a jack-of-all-trades, and master of none, don't throw in the towel. Become a master of one — or a few. You are here to fulfill a definite purpose, and it is within your power to do so. Living without purpose is like crawling around on your knees. If an infant can get up and find its way, so can you! So crawl, fall, but don't stop until you're walking! Now, start "falling" until you "stand" your way into your purpose.

Here's how to get started. Pick your top five career interests. For instance, you may enjoy cooking, as well as singing, and you are not sure which to pursue. Be scientific and experiment. Role-play. Try your hand at cooking. See if it's for you. Fully engage in the process. Don't hold back. Jump in there with both feet. Don't permit fear to arrest you and cause you to fail by omission. Fail trying! Why? With each unsuccessful attempt, you will get a valuable lesson for the next attempt. Remember, failing does not make you a failure, it makes you a student. As Les Brown says, *"If at first you do not succeed, you're running about average."* Statistics tell us that most Americans average about four professional career changes throughout their lives. Be patient and allow yourself to sample and experiment with your various interests. Your experimentation will do two things: It will eliminate those areas that you aren't really cut out for, and it will single out the area that is most in alignment with your purpose. Try something. Move. Don't get stuck in a sea of indecision. Eventually, your failures will become formulas for discovering and answering your calling.

10. Role Play

Those of us who have a family to support, and other financial obligations, are more likely to accept a role in a company that doesn't value us. But we only allow this because we don't know our purpose for being. When we come to know our purpose, we will not be defined, confined, or attached to any role not of our choosing.

For many people, a job gives them a sense of purpose. I say a sense because having a career in a field in which you don't belong may make you seem useful. But does it make you feel purposeful? There's a big difference between useful and purposeful. Many people use skills they've developed in their careers, but find that they're depleted and unsatisfied at the end of the work day. What's happening here is that they are substituting their skills for their purpose.

People like this are only scratching the surface of their potential, and yet they have even greater resources at their command. When you live from your purpose, all your gifts, skills and talent are marshaled to assist you in fulfilling your mission. On the other hand, when we elevate one skill and substitute it for our purpose, it's like driving a car with three flat tires. Sure, you can get from point A to B with one good tire, but the ride won't be enjoyable, damage will be done to the vehicle, and your passengers will have a very bumpy experience.

So don't become attached to a role that doesn't allow a clear channel for your purpose to flow through. Let your experience be the theater for your purpose, experience that allows you to stand on the stage of life and lets the true you be front and center in the giving of your gifts, skills and talents. Make living a playhouse for the star that is you!

Working through each of the above steps will get you closer to the ultimate goal: discovering what idea you are in the mind of God, or, more commonly stated, discovering your purpose. This purpose is what's wrapped up in your Designer Genes. I hope these exercises will serve as sharpening tools to make your focus clear and decisive. Some of you are already on your way to living a life of purpose, while for others these nine steps may provide an *"Aha, I see!"* moment. Either way, my aim is to help you end up at the same point: on purpose! This is where the real fun begins.

Notes:

A Life of Purpose

A spiritual life

A no-Excuse life

A life of Enjoyment

A life Triumphant

2

Your Master Plan

*"A goal is an area or object towards which play
is directed in order to score."*
– Dr. Maria Nemeth

*"Show me a person who has no goals;
it is like a parked car — it's bound to go nowhere."*
– Kevin Kitrell Ross

Begin with the End in Mind

Most Americans and people around the world admire Dr. Martin Luther King, Jr. He is certainly one of my favorite people in history. He was a leader of the Civil Rights Movement in the United States. Dr. King emerged onto the national stage in the 1960's, after Rosa Parks refused to give up her seat on a segregated bus in Birmingham, Alabama. It is said that when Rosa sat down, Martin stood up. But before circumstances thrust him into the forefront of the nationwide struggle for civil rights, Dr. King had been speaking out for those rights as a young minister. People close to Dr. King said he carried in his back pocket a plan he had for mobilizing a massive non-violent Civil Rights Movement in the nation. And so what appeared to be a spontaneous reaction by Dr. King to the bold and brave act by Rosa Parks, was actually a well thought out response by him and other leaders and activists associated with him.

Do you have a master plan for your life? Greatness is never an accident. It only appears that way to those who chose to be spectators in life, rather than Designers and active agents in life.

There is a science to bringing those dreams into visibility. Stephen Covey points out in his book, *"Seven Habits of Highly Effective People,"* that top achievers begin with the end in mind: They have a clear picture of what they wish to achieve. Do you? For example, if you would like to earn your degree, then having a picture of you marching across the stage on graduation day would be the starting point. Once you have that clear picture on the screen of your mind, print it out.

Print It Out!

I use the analogy of the computer and printer because most people can relate to it. But an earlier Biblical scripture doesn't say it much differently: *"Write the vision, make it plain on tablets, so that a herald may run with it"* (Habakkuk 2:2). When you commit your vision to paper, you are crystallizing it and making a firm impression to which you can often refer. A vision gives direction and hope for a preferable future. With a sense of direction or a target, though the archer may miss the mark (sin or make an error), with practice he is sure to hit the bull's-eye!

Get On Target!

A target is a goal. Webster defines a goal as *"an object or end that one strives to attain: an aim."* Your goal should pull you to some desired outcome and you should have fun along the way. Dr. Maria Nemeth says a goal is *"an area or object towards which play is directed in order to score."* So if you want to score big in your life and have a blast doing it, get on target and play to win!

For some, goal-setting is simple, for others it's not so easy. Here are a few tips on setting goals:

1. *Make sure that your goal is in agreement with your values and beliefs, and aligned with your purpose.* Otherwise, you will either feel you are compromising yourself, or you will be discouraged by the incongruity

of your goals to your priorities and purpose. When your goals are incongruent with your purpose, breakdown is sure to follow.

2. ***Every goal is measurable in time.*** If it's not set within a specific time frame, it's a wish, not a goal. When you pray, know exactly what you are praying for. A Science of Living principle calls us to *"be definite with the Infinite."* The Bible also tells us that we have not because we ask not, or because we pray amiss. How does one pray amiss? For example, when you go to a car dealership and say to the dealer, "I want a car," this simply isn't enough. Give it shape, color, definition, and establish an exact time frame to achieve it. Be specific, be precise. When you are definite in your goal, you are on your way to achieving what you desire.

3. ***Goals are part of the whole.*** Every goal you achieve should be one more rung on your life's ladder. Let both your long-term and your short-term goals lead you into the fulfillment of the vision that God places in your soul. As the designer of your life, you must always refer back to the entire blueprint as you work on an aspect of it. Doing so helps to place the goal in perspective. Occasionally, you may find yourself devoting entirely too much energy into achieving your goal, when it may have little to no bearing on the fulfillment of your overall purpose. By recognizing the interconnectedness of your goals to your life's overall design, you can determine its importance and how much energy you should be committing toward its fulfillment.

Design Your Day

Goals are executed through definite plans of action. Don't let it be said that you failed because you didn't have a master plan. If you don't have a plan for your life, anybody else's plan will do. Rather, let it be said that you are striving to fulfill the goals that are a part of your own Peak Performance Plan.

Are you ready to design your life that is really the life of your dreams? Would you like to pick up the pace in your overall daily productivity? Then renew your commitment to your purpose each day by setting goals. It only takes a few minutes, and yet doing so will save you a great deal of time in the long run.

I recommend that you put your "to-do list" aside for a moment and consider another model. You may be thinking, "But that works for me." To-do lists are task-driven and not purpose-driven. You may not be able to connect your daily deeds and errands back to your purpose. But when you connect your goals and tasks back to your purpose, you are more apt to fulfill them with a greater sense of urgency and commitment, not from burden, duty, and obligation. When you can clearly see that your goals are a part of your greater mission in life, your entire approach to your day is more potent. You also become more discerning as to what you allow to be a part of your Daily Design.

Here's how to get started designing your day. First, stop saying, "I've got so much to do." Rather say, "Today I 'get to' accomplish such and such." When you shift from "have to" to "get to" you move from burden, duty and obligation to privilege, opportunity and possibility. You open up an energy of excitement, rather than exhaustion. Your tasks then become your accomplishments. To get started, take a blank sheet of paper. Go ahead, grab one now so that you can get a sense of what I am saying as I describe this for you.

Now title the page "Daily Design: Today's Accomplishments." Why "Today's Accomplishments"? I choose this title so that you are consciously declaring your day to be an accomplished day from the very start. Your written word is a crystallized declaration and an honorable agreement with yourself and the universe. Declaring your day to be an accomplished one from the start lightens your mental load and compels you to approach your goals as more play than work.

Secondly, write down just underneath the title your Mission Statement. Your mission statement is that which defines and gives purpose and direction to your life. My mission, for example, is to inspire and empower everyday people to live extraordinary dreams.

This statement is posted on every one of my Daily Designs. To read about how to construct a mission statement of life and work, purchase "The Path," by Laurie Beth Jones. My mission statement provides me with the opportunity to align my daily goals with my purpose. If an opportunity presents itself that is not in alignment with my purpose, and I can't justify it being so, then I simply don't do it, and I don't recommend you do it either. If your goals are taking you in a direction other than where you have envisioned yourself to be, you are expending energy wastefully, and you will cause yourself undue stress and grief. The key to living the designer life is to channel your energy in a direction that makes an impact on your life and the world around you.

When a pebble is dropped in a pond it causes a ripple effect that extends out to the shore. With focused concentration, one is able to "reach the shore" with a single intention that is aligned with purpose. Remember, goals are measurable in time and are always definite.

Here's an example of an intention aligned with purpose: I am committed to teaching my "Design Your Life class at 3:00 p.m. at Unity of Sacramento and inviting my students to appear as guests in the coaching segment of my radio show. This goal is purpose-driven because it is in alignment with my mission of empowerment. The actions I will be taking are congruent with my purpose and mission in life.

On the air at the Unity.FM studio

In my example, I offer a structured way of Designing Your Day. To review, your daily design should include the following simple elements:

1. An affirmative title
(e.g., "Daily Design: Today's Accomplishments")

2. The Date

3. Your Mission Statement

4. Domains of Accomplishment
(e.g. Spiritual, Personal, Professional, etc.)

5. Your goal(s) for each Domain of Accomplishment.

Here is how it can look:

Daily Design
TODAY'S ACCOMPLISHMENTS

Date: _____

"My mission is to inspire everyday people to live extraordinary dreams in the context of freedom, love, and joy!"

Spiritual
Today, I see myself rising 30 minutes earlier than usual (7:00 a.m.) in order to spend quiet time in meditation and journaling.

Personal
Today I see myself having at least one "green drink" and eating other life-giving, health-affirming foods that offer me energy and vitality throughout the day.

Professional
I will meet with my business partners today at 3:00 p.m. to discuss the marketing strategy for the release of our new DVD, Liberate Your Spirit.

Financial
Today, before the close of business, I will schedule a meeting with Ms. White, my financial advisor to learn more about low risk investment opportunities that will strengthen my financial portfolio.

Community
Today before I depart from the office, I will complete individual handwritten "thank you" notes to the members of the International Peace Coalition for their participation in the King Day Celebration.

The King Day Celebration created by the International Peace Coalition made the news.

As you work to create your own version of this model, permit yourself planning time, either early in the morning or the night before, depending upon when your mind is more alert. Also, try to avoid making this a "To-Do List" by suffering it with tasks that you have no sincere intentions of achieving, or ones that could be left for another day. Remember, fifteen percent of what you do may determine how well the remaining eighty-five percent will turn out. Don't concentrate on the eighty-five percent that doesn't make a difference, but rather the fifteen percent that does. Keep your list lean, inviting and achievable.

The best feeling in the world is to have lived a day you planned for. Even better is when a "pleasant surprise" shows up, a surprise you couldn't plan for. This makes life even sweeter.

These bonuses usually come to those who have an orderly consciousness, represented by a "Daily Design." As Napoleon Hill so aptly pointed out many years ago, *"What the mind of man can conceive and believe, it can achieve."* By stating your goal in the positive, you are presenting your mind with a very definite image. This image is your target, the area or object towards which you direct your joyful efforts in order to score. Your work should be joyful. As Kahlil Gibran has said, *"Your work is love made visible."* Your goals should energize, impel and compel you into every right and highest action.

Work with this simple method and watch yourself make significant progress toward your goals. Having a Daily Design and setting goals that are in alignment with your purpose is the best way to leverage yourself for maximum and meaningful achievement in life. Never have a day without a master plan. You never know when someone will sit down so that you can stand up!

Notes:

(2) Construct a Mission Statement
of life + work, read

  The Path by Laurie Beth Jones

(4) Daily Design :

Domains of Accomplishments

  Spiritual

  Personal - Health

  Personal - Relationship(s), Family

  Community - Service

  Financial

(3) Goals in Each Domain :

(1) [Vision Board]

3

Got the Picture?

*"A man's life is dyed the color
of his imagination."*
– Marcus Aurelius

*"Those who dream never sleep.
Even wide awake, every achievement is
but an anchored dream."*
– Kevin Kitrell Ross

There are so many ways I could offer to support you with Living the Designer Life. It's important to have a variety of approaches to designing the life of your dreams. There is no one way that works for everyone. Depending upon your personality, you may resist creating the "Daily Design" (a.k.a. "Today's Accomplishments List"). Some people feel overwhelmed at just the thought of enumerating their goals. Yet, though they avoid creating <u>Peak Performance Plans</u> or writing things down, life somehow brings them back to it.

If you feel challenged by this approach, practice it until you reach a comfort level. You might try creating a "Vision Board." This is a large board — cardboard, probably — upon

Here is my actual vision board that I used to manifest my appearance on the Oprah Show and other amazing successes, including executive producing my own TV special, Liberate Your Spirit.

which you paste or tape photos, drawings, paintings — things which please and inspire you. One of the late comedian Flip Wilson's frequent lines was "What you see is what you get." He said it flippantly (no pun intended), but nothing could be further from the truth. As a child, I was fascinated by stories of pirates and treasure hunts. I would root for the "good guys" — or so I thought they were — to find the right map (sometimes there was a decoy) that would lead them to the buried treasure. This technique is not much different, except there is more than one "treasure" to seek. What we are seeking to unearth are the treasures in you.

With the Vision Board — or treasure map, if you prefer — we are able to visually see our heart's desires in pictures. This might also be called "pictured prayer." The Designer Life calls for the designer to exercise his or her imagination.

I call the imagination a "nation of images," or "a world of pictures." It is how you view the world in your mind's eye. Imagination is a powerful faculty of mind that can shape substance. It helps you to cut out from the immaterial world the images you desire to experience in the material world.

As you work with the Vision Board, you must use your power to visualize. Perhaps you recall the exercise in the first chapter of this book, wherein I asked you to see yourself in the infinite mind of God. What did you see? Were you able to see anything? This exercise was designed, in part, to stimulate your imagination. Those mental images you hold dominantly in your consciousness are the foundation for what you will achieve in life.

If you recall, in Chapter 2, when I stated the goal for each domain, I began some of the sentences with the words, "I see myself..." Seeing yourself being, doing, and having, the life of your dreams is the precursor to actually achieving it. Thus, as the designer, you must use your imagination to see your world and yourself precisely as you wish for it to be — without discrimination, doubt or prejudice of any sort. Simply give your imagination permission to put your dreams in picture form.

This technique requires that you activate your spiritual faculty, your faith. Yes, faith. Faith enables you to "see" in the dark. According to Charles Fillmore, co-founder of the Unity Movement, in his book *Revealing Word* *"Faith is a deep inner knowing that what is sought is already ours for taking. Faith is the perceiving power of the mind linked with the power to shape substance. Spiritual assurance; the power to do the seemingly impossible. It is a magnetic power that draws unto us our heart's desire from the invisible spiritual substance."*

To use the technique of vision boarding, you must follow the steps for assembling your map — or collage, if you will. As you begin to create your Vision Board, let your faith guide you to believe that what you desire is already on its way. Your impulse and drive will help you to bring it forth. Move forward and trust this inner-knowing, and fearlessly and creatively map your own destiny.

Remember, vision boarding is simply the process of visualizing exactly what you want. The clearer you can see it as a reality, the sooner it will become real. The magical part about vision boarding is that you don't have to know where the desired object or opportunity will come from. In other words, you do not have to figure out how they will occur or be achieved. Once you declare what it is you truly desire, the results will astound you and come from both expected and unexpected ways. From gifts, unexpected letters in the mail, a big break, money left in a will, or a "seeming" chance encounter, the results are a glad surprise.

I was introduced to this method as a child growing up in Chicago. Since then, I have used every technique in this book to design the life of my dreams. I have used vision boarding to help me manifest many of my dreams.

Here's a short list:

1. Having an amazing wife and three incredible children.

2. Meeting both President Nelson Mandela and His Holiness, The Dalai Lama at a conference in South Africa.

3. Serving as the Senior Minister of the flagship church, Unity of Sacramento.

4. Having my DVD Liberate Your Spirit published internationally by the same company that released, "The Secret."

5. Served over 1,000 teens through my own charity, Teen Dream Camp.

Here on the set of Liberate Your Spirit, I am interviewing James Trapp and Michael Bernard Beckwith.

6. Inducted into the Preachers Hall of Fame at Morehouse College.

7. Celebrating 13 years as a life coach with successful clients throughout the world.

8. Having the most amazing friendships that have spanned over 20 years.

9. Enjoying vacations spread across four different continents.

10. Winning two Humanitarian Awards and several proclamations for peace building and community outreach.

The list could be longer, but those 10 examples illustrate that this process works. As my mentor and teacher, Dr. Johnnie Colemon, says, *"It works if you work it!"* And that means you!

So, are you ready to work it? Start by gathering the following materials.

Materials

- Tri-fold standing display or poster board
- Magazines
- Scissors
- Pictures, news-clippings
- Stick glue
- Journal, manila folders, card stock paper or creation box
- Markers, crayons or other writing materials
- Affirmations and goal list easily accessible to transfer to front/back of treasure map
- Stickers, glitter and construction paper
- Stencils, rulers, transfer letters
- Photographs of yourself

Instructions

1. Begin with a Prayer of Acceptance. Acknowledge the Source for giving you the Master plan for your life. Accept it gladly and proceed to bring it into view.

2. Find an open space to lay out your magazines and materials (table or floor), and have all your materials on hand. Begin to add your pictures and affirmations — at random or by category. Use glue or tape to paste the photos. Take markers, glitter, and other decorative items to make your board come alive. Above all, have fun in the process!

3. Take a clean sheet of paper or a few blank pages in your journal to brainstorm what you would like to manifest in your life. The following are the seven primary domains to consider:

Spiritual	Professional	Personal
Health/Wellness	Recreational/Social	Financial
Relational		

Write a list of all you wish to manifest. I repeat, ALL! It is important that you do not discriminate against yourself. Acknowledge any inner conversation that may attempt to discourage you, and say, "Not this time." Then continue with your brainstorming process. The list you produce will be very important as it will serve as the blueprint for your Vision Board.

4. Cut out the photographs, settings and words from the magazines you've gathered which correspond with your list of desires. For example, if you want to create peace and harmony in your life, select images that evoke a peaceful feeling in you. You may also select photographs of yourself, those you don't mind cropping. For example, if you are working to develop your physique, and you see a body image in a magazine, cut it out and paste a photo of your own head onto the shoulders of the body from the magazine. Select every word and picture carefully and make sure that each image and word evokes a powerful feeling.

5. Once you have completed your Vision Board, review it, admire, and bless it. By doing so, you change it into a sacred and magnetic tool of attraction for helping you realize your heart's desires. It will also help you to repel anything in you that is not in sync with those desires.

6. Upon completion of your board, find a place in your home where you (and only you) can see it every day. This place should be your private sanctuary; a place for your personal reflection and devotion. There should be a consistent positive flow of energy where your board is kept. And when you enter this place for your private quiet time, affirm aloud each wish and desire depicted on your board.

Now that you have created this very special tool, use it. Trust the process and see yourself having, doing, and being all that you have desired. This is the surest way to its attainment.

Vision Boarding Tips

1. Use bright colors on your board. Grays and blacks cause a dismal atmosphere, and are not conducive to helping you realize the healthy aspects of your heart's desires. Remember what the old song said: "Accentuate the positive and eliminate the negative."

2. Don't add a specific someone onto your board if (a) you don't want to manifest him or her, or (b) they

don't want you to manifest them. This is just asking for trouble and can make your creative waters murky! (An image of someone you don't know is fine.)

3. Don't let your collage get outdated. If you lose interest in your board, discard it or design a new one. You will find that you can use this process the rest of your life. With each new vision board you design, the more possibilities of success you will invite into your life.

Notes:

Notes:

4

Packaging Your Purpose

*"Act the way you want to be and soon
you'll be the way you act."*
– Dr. David Montogmery

*"Go into life looking good, smelling good
and feeling good, and life will reward you generously for
having done so."*
– Kevin Kitrell Ross

No matter how gigantic your mission is or how well you have planned, if you haven't learned to communicate it in a way that others will receive it, it will remain wrapped up in you. Style is the manner in which you present yourself to life. While the gift is the important thing, how well that gift is wrapped often determines whether it is ever opened — or when it is opened.

The old clichés are true: *"You must dress for success," "You must look the part," "You must be able to make a statement without saying a word."* There's something about a well-dressed person that communicates confidence. The way you dress and carry yourself in public tells people a lot about who you are. Teddy Gunther, makeover specialist and image consultant to the stars (i.e. Will Smith and The Rock), recalls a time when an insurance salesman came on a sales call to her office. The entire time he was making his sales pitch, she couldn't help but notice that his nails were badly kept. While it might have been the best deal of her life, she didn't sign with him because of his own careless grooming habits.

I use this example because while you look at personal style and relate it to fashion, it is important to recognize that how you appear is a reflection of your practice of self care or lack thereof.

The time you give to preparing yourself for the day is an opportunity to love yourself, appreciate yourself, encourage yourself, and celebrate yourself. You are not merely dressing yourself, you are "clothing" yourself with the right mental attitude and spirit necessary to face your life victoriously. Take pride in your appearance, not only because of what you are wearing, but because of what you are exuding.

We can block ourselves from Living the Life Triumphant because of what we don't know about ourselves. Sometimes the messenger can short circuit his own message. I recall when as a college student at Morehouse, I was invited to be the guest speaker for the pre-college summer academy students. I was proud of the message I delivered to the

Here I am with my Morehouse College mentor and friend, Dr. Lawrence E. Carter, Sr. years after the "yellow socks" story.

students. However, when I asked my mentor, Dean Carter, for his reaction to my speech, he said, "Your socks spoke so loud that I didn't hear a word you said." I was crushed. I had thought my attire was well-suited (no pun intended) for this special occasion: business suit, white shirt, yellow tie, yellow handkerchief, and — you guessed it — yellow socks! If this were a career speaking opportunity, it may have cost me a great deal more than just Dr. Carter's feedback.

How might a lack of fashion sense by the messenger cause dismissal of the message? How can you improve your style and appearance to make a greater impact in your workplace and elsewhere? In my Designer Life Workshops, I include consultants to advise on the importance of personal style and appearance as it relates to Living the Designer Life. Participants are actually able to receive a wardrobe edit on the spot. In this book, however, I provide you with a collection of tools, tips and reminders on how you can improve your own image. Many of which have come directly from Sonia Jacobson and Teddy Gunther, two professional image consultants from Florida who have helped both celebrities and everyday job applicants to select wardrobes that enhanced their personal style, highlighted their heart's message, and accommodated their budgets. They taught me that it takes about three seconds to assess someone visually on a first impression. And there is no second time to make a first impression. It's important that we make sure we are appropriately "suited for success."

While I don't wish to place an imbalanced emphasis on the way you dress, it is a factor that still remains relevant in how you and your purpose my be perceived and received by the world. Your personal style is an unspoken language and you are constantly being judged and misjudged by what messages are sent through what you are wearing. In the pursuit of your dreams, make sure to put your best foot forth.

Here we go...

You Can Always Improve Your Image

My early childhood mentor, Dr. Gwindol P. Tate, often said, *"Good, better, best; never let it rest until your good is better and better is best. And you can always better your best yet."*

Your image is both how you see yourself and how you project yourself to the world. How you dress informs people what you think about yourself, and, perhaps, what you think of them. For instance, going to a business meeting in blue jeans and a t-shirt would probably tell your client that you didn't think enough about them to dress appropriately. Chances are, you will not leave a favorable impression.

Please note that every person has his own unique personal style and comfort level in how he or she chooses to dress. These words are not designed to discourage you from having a wardrobe that honors who you are or your uniqueness. It is, however, important to ensure that you are "situationally relevant." That is, how you present yourself and your purpose should be suitable for the situation that you wish to be successful in.

On this topic, an internal quality that gets to be activated and developed, is flexibility. Your ability to be flexible, will allow you to be coachable and as such, you will be able to adapt to a variety of experiences which will qualify you for opportunities beyond your wildest imagination.

While it may seem odd, I have grown because of the feedback I have received about my wardrobe. You may recall my "yellow sock story." Since that day, I have committed myself to being open, flexible, coachable and to practicing a formula I devised with my lifelong friend, Dr. David Montgomery, called, ARFI (pronounced ar-fee). It is an acronym for Always Room for Improvement. Yes, you can always better your best. Car manufacturers are constantly at the drawing board crafting newer, faster, sleeker models of automobiles. Similarly, we should focus on presenting ourselves in the best possible manner. To use a formulation by the great Scottish poet Robert Burns, we should strive to *"see ourselves as others see us."* If we could do that, Burns says, it would free us from *"many a blunder...and foolish notion."*

You might need to practice ARFI if...

a. You have worn the same hairstyle for the last five or more years.

b. The colors you wear don't project the mood, attitude, or spirit you wish to portray.

c. You are unable to close on a deal though you have the skills required.

d. You are not called back for a second interview.

e. People avoid conversing with you at networking functions or formal dinners.

f. Your clothes are too tight or too loose.

g. You're told that you're extremely talented, but you are never selected for an audition.

h. You never receive compliments on your appearance.

Here is a list of questions and ideas that will help you become more aware of your self-image:

1. When was the last time you read something about fashion and/or the best way to visually present yourself? If you can't remember, it's been too long.

2. When was the last time you considered updating your hairstyle?

3. When was the last time you had a facial consultation (i.e. skin care, make-up, etc)?

4. What is your fitness routine?

5. What regimen do you use for your overall skin care?

6. How often do you attend to your nails?

7. What is your dental hygiene?

8. What condition are your "best" pair of shoes right now?

Practice the Four Basic Fashion Rules

Consider yourself a canvas, and your clothes should grace you as works of art. There are some basic rules that you (man or woman) can follow relating to your wardrobe.

1. Condition

Make sure your clothing is in good condition. Frilly, stained, dull (as in color), or damaged clothing will be recognized within seconds and communicate an image of carelessness. Always check the condition of the clothes you consider buying, and the clothes you consider wearing day by day.

2. Fashionable/Classic

There are two basic styles in clothing: fashionable or classic. Decide which of the two you consider appropriate for a particular occasion. Of course, sometimes what is classic may also be fashionable, and vice versa. Although an item of clothing may be fashionable, it may not be suitable for where you are going or what you will be doing.

3. Quality

Although you have to stay within your budget, it's better to select one item of quality clothing than a few inferior pieces. Build your wardrobe one piece at a time. You can tell the quality of an item of clothing by the texture of the fabric. For example, an item that is 100 percent cotton wears better over time than a synthetic fabric. Also, the proper fit is important.

Buy brands that have a reputation for quality. Such a brand, for example, is Brioni, which manufactures men's suits. In a Brioni suit the hand-stitching around the lapel and the ultra-fine threads in the fabric stand out. Levi's jeans are known for their durability and unique metal reinforcements near the zipper.

The best you can afford may come from Sax Fifth Avenue or a TJ Maxx. where they sell quality brand name items for less. And here's a secret among the well-dressed among us: vintage stores. At one of these stores you can sometimes find the very best quality clothing at rock bottom prices. How come? Because the clothing is pre-owned. Don't be fooled into disregarding an item of clothing because it has been pre-owned. Well-to-do people frequently change their wardrobe though it may still be in excellent condition. So consider yourself in "good company" at a vintage store. And to ensure that you're looking like a million dollars in a Gucci suit that you purchased for fifty dollars at a vintage shop, take it to a tailor/seamstress and spend another $20 to alter it for a perfect fit.

The point is to get the best value for your money. Higher quality clothing fit better, look better and last longer.

4. Styling Your Outfits

If you're a busy individual who doesn't have time to be fashion-conscious, there are some simple things you can do to make sure you always show up looking your best.

a. Read fashion magazines. For women, try Vogue. For men, try GQ (Gentlemen's Quarterly). You will not only see great fashion, but you will get time-saving tips to help you look like the star you are. If you like what you see, and it's appropriate for the occasion, "copy it." Again, consider your budget. You may even have similar items in your wardrobe. Use their styling as a guide.

b. Use a fashion-conscious person to help you. Did you know, for instance, that at major department stores like Bloomingdales and Lord and Taylor there are personnel available to coordinate entire outfits to suit your taste — absolutely free? You can even bring items of your own clothing to the store and coordinate outfits with items that are available in their inventory.

Also, ask a friend who you feel has good taste in fashion to do a "closet edit" with you. A closet/wardrobe edit is when you open your wardrobe for inspection and critique. A trusted friend will tell you what he or she feels is not flattering to you, or is simply "played out." Your friend may even be willing to help you co-ordinate several outfits.

You and your friend might spread out several "put together" outfits so that they are easy to see. A "put together" look is an outfit that is ready to roll from head to toe, including accessories. Turn on some music and model each outfit. Make sure you look and feel great in your outfit. Have your friend photograph you in each outfit. If you have a Polaroid camera, it's preferable for this purpose; it gives you prints immediately. However, I do recognize that digital cameras are more commonly used these days, so feel free to take digital pictures. Either print them or ensure that they can be easily accessed for reference.

Photograph each outfit and assemble the prints into an album or electronic album if you went digital. Now you'll have your very own catalogue of "put together looks" for every occasion.

Divide the book by time of day and occasion. So from now on, when you're ready to step out, just match what you wear with one of the photos in the book, and you'll know you're going to look great. Update your book a minimum of two times a year to make sure you're current with trends and friends. Just like the combo meal concept. Easy, convenient, priced right, and ready to go.

Every day you deserve to take life with style. It's important that you look and feel your best! What you wear tells about you. Your personal grooming communicates to the world how you feel about yourself. Let the world know, without saying a word, that you feel great! Your appearance announces, *"I am a force to be reckoned with in the universe."* Let all who see you know you're one of a kind, an original, and from head to toe, inside and out, everything about you is purposeful, a product of conscious design.

Notes:

5

Design Your Legacy

"I would rather walk into hell on purpose than to stumble into heaven by following the crowd."
– Dr. Benjamin Elijah

"Give yourself permission to be great!"
– Kevin Kitrell Ross

Living the Designer Life is incomplete without giving selfless service. While this book offers techniques that empower you to demonstrate the consciousness to attract your desires, be mindful that the Divine Design is all about what you give, not what you take.

When Dr. Marian Wright Edelman, founder and president of The Children's Defense Fund, said, *"Service is the rent that we pay for being on this earth,"* she had no idea that they would resonate with such volume in my soul. As a boy of fourteen, I agonized over the deplorable condition of the world, which was unusual for me because I was raised to look for the good that was present in every situation. But after hearing a compelling orator and national leader spout out a litany of the world's ills, I considered myself helpless, and the world a hopeless cause. I was left with many questions, including, "Can I make a difference?"

Initially, when reviewing what I considered to be a hopeless situation, I came to a chilling conclusion: One person alone cannot change the world. I used to think so. My hero, Dr. King, did. But even the great Dr. King did not act alone. I realized that if I were to make a difference, I needed to return to my once sunny outlook. And I vowed that I would use my influence to help change the world. I pledged to devote my life toward that end from that day forward.

I began to design my legacy of service. But how would I go about it? What cause would I take on? To what great cause would I devote my life? When I heard Dr. Edelman's words, I realized that service is a necessary aspect of life. I learned that service is a state of being, an aspect of good character, and the by-product of having a healthy spirituality. I concluded that there is no one way, no one group of people or special cause, that I had to represent, so long as I "paid my rent."

Each payment in service I made on behalf of any great cause, I was doing for the entire human household. Each and every day, I look for an opportunity to serve, to justify my usefulness on the planet.

There are many "placeholders" for whom we pay a high price, either in money or in services. I'm referring to those who are occupying space but are making no contribution toward improving the lives of those around them. You may know some of these people — and you must ask yourself, "Am I one of them?" They are takers, not givers. To avoid being a taker, pay your rent! Following are several ways you can serve others and increase your personal worth at the same time.

Do Something That Comes Easy

As I mentioned earlier, there are no set rules for whom or how you must serve. According to Dr. Martin Luther King, Jr., *"You only need a heart full of love and a soul generated by grace."* So avoid starting with some global humanitarian mission. Inevitably, by taking on larger than life projects, you may feel overwhelmed and burned out, or you will feel inadequate and lose your motivation. Start from where you are with what you have. For instance, if you are a musician, perhaps you should volunteer your time as a choir director or as a voice coach. You could entertain seniors on weekends. There's no rule that says you can't enjoy yourself while giving to others. Besides, you will experience a deep sense of satisfaction and gratitude when you give of yourself.

The more you are engaging your gifts, the richer they become and the more fulfilled and accomplished you feel as an individual. Someone once said, *"Give 'til it hurts."* But my motto is, *"Give 'til it feels great!"*

Serve Unconsciously

Every day you draw breath is a day your "rent" is due. We inhale and exhale naturally and effortlessly, unconscious of the process. What if we adopted this same attitude to giving? Move beyond counting community service hours. Instead of your service being a trophy you mount for others to see, let it become a contribution that sinks deep into your character. Giving should not be a chore, but something inherent in who you are. Like breathing, you will begin to do it unconsciously.

Stay in Your Lane

While you enjoy the rewards of your service, those you serve will enjoy it as well. As I said before, serve in whatever capacity you are best suited. While I enjoy and am gifted at working with teenagers, I am better skilled working on their behalf, through organizing, programming, fundraising and mobilizing. Today I am the co-founder and President of Teen Dream

Camp with my wife Anita. Teen Dream Camp (www.teen-dreamcamop.org) is a 501 (c) (3) tax exempt organization designed to interrupt pattens of teen self sabotage and suicide, by launching the dreams in the hearts of teens. Well over 1,000 teens have been positively impacted by our efforts and we have raised nearly half a million dollars to benefit teens since 1994.

What area are you best suited for? Chances are, the skills for which you shine in your professional work are the same ones that will enable you to shine as you serve. Verify your effectiveness by observing those you serve. If you are in doubt, most service organizations offer assessment tools that will help you determine the right "lane" for you.

My wife and I with a group of Teen Dream Camp graduates.

Just remember, some people are best suited for indirect care, usually in some advocacy or administrative role. Others are better suited for interacting face-to-face with people. Nevertheless, if you are in the right service lane, you will gain greater satisfaction, as will those impacted by your service.

Self Service

While service is other-focused, it is extremely important that you periodically check in with yourself to replenish your soul. Your commitment to being a caretaker, mentor, tutor, or volunteer, will likely be in addition to a full-time job, your roles as spouse, parent, or significant other. It is key that you take time to rejuvenate, so that you are always giving from a cup that is running over and not from an empty well.

If you have ever flown in a plane, you've heard the flight attendant announce, during the emergency briefing, *"In the event of an emergency, place your oxygen mask on yourself before you attempt to place one on a minor."* By taking care of yourself first, you are sustaining the soul that serves.

Having a balanced diet, proper rest, and time for reflection, are all part of giving to yourself. When you have experienced the joy of serving yourself with love and affection, sharing it with others won't be a chore, but a thrill.

Take the time to compile a journal. Write down insights as you reflect on your encounters with those whom you serve. Keep drawings and letters that children give you. They will motivate you when the days seem longer and tougher than usual. Pray for strength to be in your best health and attitude as you give back to God by giving back to God's children.

You are a Legacy in the Making

Everyday that you live your life in congruence with your purpose and passion, you are designing your legacy. It is a powerful statement about your life that people identify your name with greatness, both while you are on this earth and after you make your exit from this life.

Dark clouds evaporate with every enthusiastic person I meet, those who have found a way to brighten up their corner of the earth through selfless service. This is our greatest asset, and it pays great dividends. You can deliberately serve your way into immortality. Be on purpose. You've got Designer Genes — the stuff that genius is made of. Leave your thumbprint of excellence on the world. You will surely have designed and lived the Life Triumphant.

Here I am with Dr. Brenda Wade being interviewed for my success secrets.

Margaret Mead, the great anthropologist, said it best: *"Never doubt that a small group of thoughtful, committed citizens can change the world. Indeed, it is the only thing that ever has."*

I always strive to be among this group of thoughtful, committed citizens and I invite you to join me.

Dreams in the Making

By Eric Ovid Donaldson and Daniel Tucker

If when adversity should strike in your life,

And you can look beyond the setbacks and strife,

If neither sorrow, nor grief can challenge your belief,

And you can see the victory that lies in defeat,

And mistakes and errors you don't repeat,

If you are willing to pursue your goal and your dreams,

No matter how far in distance they may seem,

And you refuse to relent,

No matter the trials and tribulations sent,

And if you can see all of the beauty that lies all around you,

And you know that the love of God surrounds you,

And you can love yourself,

And believe in yourself,

Then all of the things that you hope for, and fight for,

and pray for shall be there fore the taking,

For your dreams my friend,

were always in the making.

Order your DVD copy of...

Liberate Your Spirit

with Kevin Kitrell Ross

In Liberate Your Spirit, renowned author, speaker, and minister Kevin Kitrell Ross interviews three powerhouse spiritual leaders to unveil the true strength and potential hidden within each of us.

Through gripping tales of triumph and transformation, Ross unveils a new paradigm that offers success and fulfillment where traditional theology and outdated concepts of God have failed. You'll hear from:

- Bestselling author and modern mystic Michael Bernard Beckwith who details how he turned from agnostic beliefs when stunning visions led him to the dynamic healing teachings of the New Thought movement.

- Inspirational speaker and President of Unity Worldwide Ministries James Trapp, who reveals how he went from successful lawyer to extreme drug abuse and lost "everything"--before discovering his true path.

- Prolific author and founder of the Kansas City Center for Spiritual Living, Chris Michaels, who bravely shares how he was contemplating suicide when he "stumbled" into an inclusive spiritual community that saved his life.

ORDER YOURS TODAY AT: WWW.LIBERATEYOURSPIRIT.ORG

.